I0211140

Coloring Book
The Sun Catherine

by
Astrid Listner

Illustrated by
Susanne Auschill

Copyright © 2015 Creative-Story, Munich (Germany)

Astrid Listner
Coloring Book - The Sun Catherine,
Creative books for sunny adventures, vol. 1,
Illustrated by Susanne Auschill

Creative-Story
Safferlingstr. 5 / 134
D-80634 Munich
Germany
Tel.: +49 (0)89 / 12 11 14 66
Fax: +49 (0)89 / 12 11 14 68
info@creative-story.com
www.creative-story.com

Cover-design, layout and typesetting:
Creative-Web-Projects, Munich

ISBN: 978-3-95964-006-0

Legal Notices
All rights reserved. No portion of this book may be reproduced, stored in a retrieval system or transmitted in any form or by any means - electronic, mechanical, photo-copying, recording or otherwise - without written permission of the publisher.

Acknowledgement by the Author
My special thanks go to my editor, publisher and good friend. Thank you for your creative power, tenacity and genuine friendship.

For Mom & Dad

The Sun Catherine

© 2015 Creative-Story, Munich

A. Listner / S. Auschill:
Coloring Book - The Sun Catherine

© 2015 Creative-Story, Munich

A. Listner / S. Auschill:
Coloring Book - The Sun Catherine

© 2015 Creative-Story, Munich

A. Listner / S. Auschill:
Coloring Book - The Sun Catherine

© 2015 Creative-Story, Munich

A. Listner / S. Auschill:
Coloring Book - The Sun Catherine

© 2015 Creative-Story, Munich

A. Listner / S. Auschill:
Coloring Book - The Sun Catherine

© 2015 Creative-Story, Munich

A. Listner / S. Auschill:
Coloring Book - The Sun Catherine

© 2015 Creative-Story, Munich

A. Listner / S. Auschill:
Coloring Book - The Sun Catherine

© 2015 Creative-Story, Munich

A. Listner / S. Auschill:
Coloring Book - The Sun Catherine

© 2015 Creative-Story, Munich

A. Listner / S. Auschill:
Coloring Book - The Sun Catherine

© 2015 Creative-Story, Munich

A. Listner / S. Auschill:
Coloring Book - The Sun Catherine

© 2015 Creative-Story, Munich

A. Listner / S. Auschill:
Coloring Book - The Sun Catherine

© 2015 Creative-Story, Munich

A. Listner / S. Auschill:
Coloring Book - The Sun Catherine

© 2015 Creative-Story, Munich

A. Listner / S. Auschill:
Coloring Book - The Sun Catherine

© 2015 Creative-Story, Munich

A. Listner / S. Auschill:
Coloring Book - The Sun Catherine

© 2015 Creative-Story, Munich

A. Listner / S. Auschill:
Coloring Book - The Sun Catherine

© 2015 Creative-Story, Munich

A. Listner / S. Auschill:
Coloring Book - The Sun Catherine

© 2015 Creative-Story, Munich

A. Listner / S. Auschill:
Coloring Book - The Sun Catherine

© 2015 Creative-Story, Munich

A. Listner / S. Auschill:
Coloring Book - The Sun Catherine

© 2015 Creative-Story, Munich

A. Listner / S. Auschill:
Coloring Book - The Sun Catherine

© 2015 Creative-Story, Munich

A. Listner / S. Auschill:
Coloring Book - The Sun Catherine

© 2015 Creative-Story, Munich

A. Listner / S. Auschill:
Coloring Book - The Sun Catherine

© 2015 Creative-Story, Munich

A. Listner / S. Auschill:
Coloring Book - The Sun Catherine

© 2015 Creative-Story, Munich

A. Listner / S. Auschill:
Coloring Book - The Sun Catherine

© 2015 Creative-Story, Munich

A. Listner / S. Auschill:
Coloring Book - The Sun Catherine

© 2015 Creative-Story, Munich

A. Listner / S. Auschill:
Coloring Book - The Sun Catherine

© 2015 Creative-Story, Munich

A. Listner / S. Auschill:
Coloring Book - The Sun Catherine

© 2015 Creative-Story, Munich

A. Listner / S. Auschill:
Coloring Book - The Sun Catherine

© 2015 Creative-Story, Munich

A. Listner / S. Auschill:
Coloring Book - The Sun Catherine

© 2015 Creative-Story, Munich

A. Listner / S. Auschill:
Coloring Book - The Sun Catherine

© 2015 Creative-Story, Munich

A. Listner / S. Auschill:
Coloring Book - The Sun Catherine

© 2015 Creative-Story, Munich

A. Listner / S. Auschill:
Coloring Book - The Sun Catherine

© 2015 Creative-Story, Munich

A. Listner / S. Auschill:
Coloring Book - The Sun Catherine

© 2015 Creative-Story, Munich

A. Listner / S. Auschill:
Coloring Book - The Sun Catherine

© 2015 Creative-Story, Munich

A. Listner / S. Auschill:
Coloring Book - The Sun Catherine

© 2015 Creative-Story, Munich

A. Listner / S. Auschill:
Coloring Book - The Sun Catherine

© 2015 Creative-Story, Munich

A. Listner / S. Auschill:
Coloring Book - The Sun Catherine

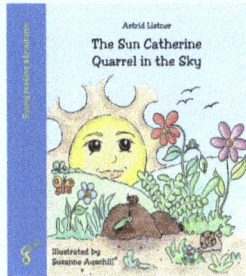

The Sun Catherine - Quarrel in the Sky
(Sunny reading adventures, vol. 1)
ISBN 978-3-95964-005-3

The adventures of

Catherine, Felix and William

continue in volume 2:

The Cloud Felix - Why Friends are Important
(Sunny reading adventures, vol. 2)
ISBN 978-3-95964-045-9

Coloring Book - The Cloud Felix
ISBN 978-3-95964-046-6

www.ingramcontent.com/pod-product-compliance
Lightning Source LLC
Chambersburg PA
CBHW050257090426
42734CB00022B/3487